Ocean
watch

Written by
MARTYN BRAMWELL
Consultant
DR PHILIP WHITFIELD

DK

A Dorling Kindersley Book

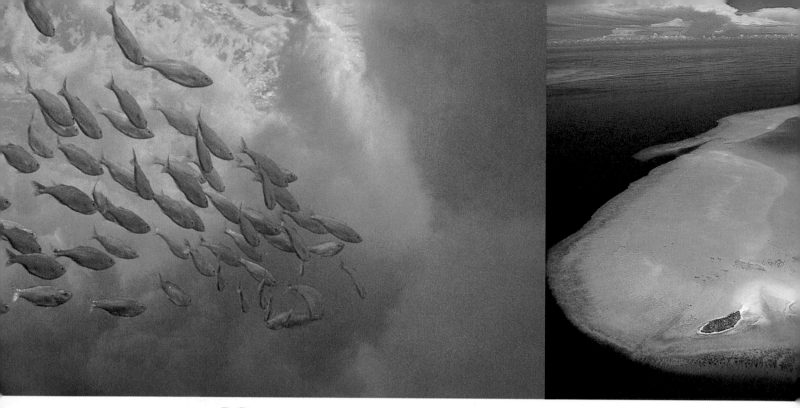

Dorling DK Kindersley

LONDON, NEW YORK, SYDNEY, DELHI,
PARIS, MUNICH, and JOHANNESBURG

Project Editor Marek Walisiewicz
Art Editors Janet Allis, Mark Regardsoe
Senior Editor Fran Jones
Managing Editor Sue Grabham
Senior Managing Art Editor Julia Harris
Picture Researcher Michèle Faram
Production Kate Oliver and Chris Avgherinos
Senior DTP Designer Andrew O'Brien
US Editor Chuck Wills

First American Edition 2001
01 02 03 04 05 10 9 8 7 6 5 4 3 2

Published in the United States by
Dorling Kindersley Publishing, Inc.
95 Madison Avenue, New York, New York 10016

Copyright © 2001 Dorling Kindersley Limited

Library of Congress Cataloging-in-Publication Data

Bramwell, Martyn.
  Make a difference. Oceanwatch / written by Martyn Bramwell ;
consultant, Philip Whitfield -- 1st American ed.
  p. cm.
  ISBN 0-7894-6894-8
  1. Ocean--Environmental aspects--Juvenile literature. [1. Ocean. 2.
Oceanography.] I. Title

GC21.5 .B72 2001
333.91'6416--dc21

00-043015

Reproduced by Colourscan, Singapore
Printed and bound by L.E.G.O., Italy.

See our complete catalog at
www.dk.com

Contents

Introduction

The oceans affect our lives every day – whether we live on the coast or far inland. They control the weather and prevent our planet from overheating. But it is only recently that modern technology has enabled us to understand the workings of the oceans and to chart their darkest depths. It was not always this way. For thousands of years the seas were a mysterious and unknown world – stormy and dangerous, but endlessly fascinating. However, during the second half of the 20th century, people began to enter this underwater world – diving suits, submarines, and scientific submersibles allowed scientists to explore beneath the waves, while sonar, satellites, and other technologies provided new ways of unlocking the oceans' secrets.

Today, our knowledge of the oceans is growing at a tremendous pace – but this knowledge has also revealed some startling truths. Through ignorance, carelessness, and sometimes greed, we have been damaging the marine environment for years. Chemicals from agriculture and industry are now spread far and wide through the oceans. Some whales and fish have been hunted almost to extinction, and climate changes caused by a polluted atmosphere may cause sea levels to rise and cover hundreds of the world's islands and low-lying coasts. Fortunately, our increased knowledge also means that we can do something about these problems – and if we work together we can halt the damage and even repair some of it.

Already, scientists, conservation groups, and ordinary people across the globe are demanding that governments pass stronger laws to ensure that the seas and their inhabitants are protected, and that industries everywhere clean up their acts. But we still have a long way to go. On some of the main issues, such as global warming, experts do not always agree about the problems and what should be done. This book explains the key issues that surround the problems and presents a clear picture of what is at stake.

"Freshwater and marine habitats, especially coral reefs, are very vulnerable."

UNITED NATIONS ENVIRONMENT PROGRAM, EARTHSCAN 2000

Because the oceans are so vast, it is easy to feel there is little we can do. But individuals can make a difference. In this book, there are suggestions for ways you can play an active role, and experiments to provide firsthand experience of some of the scientific issues. Day in the Life journals describe the work of experts in the field, while letters from young people around the world reveal their concerns for the environment. If we act now, we can all help to safeguard the future of the oceans.

ONE OCEAN

THE PACIFIC, ATLANTIC, INDIAN, ARCTIC, AND ANTARCTIC OCEANS ARE ALL LINKED IN ONE VAST MASS OF WATER. Together they have a huge effect on our lives. They control the weather and prevent our planet from overheating. The oceans supply most of the oxygen that we breathe, and give us great riches of food and minerals. We should start to take care of them, for the sake of the future.

Hawaiian flagtails (main
picture) and Atlantic herring
(inset) are both important
links in their local food
chains. They also provide
valuable food resources
for people. But there is a
big difference. The flagtail
population is still healthy,
while in some areas the
herring have almost been
wiped out by overfishing.

Worlds in *motion*

The oceans are never still. Every day, the tides rise and fall, and all year round great rivers of water, called currents, swirl around the oceans. The tides are caused by the pull of the Moon as it passes overhead, but the currents are pushed along by the winds, which get their energy from the heat of the Sun. Scientists are worried that global warming (the heating of the Earth's surface) could alter winds and currents, melt the polar ice caps, and upset Earth's weather systems and climate zones.

Arctic Ocean
The smallest of the oceans is covered with thick ice.

Pacific Ocean
The world's largest ocean, its deepest point is more than 6.8 miles (11 km) below the surface.

Power of the sea

Out at sea, waves usually just rise and fall like giant ripples. They only form "whitecaps" when driven by strong winds. But when a wave surges up a beach, the water piles up until it topples over. Curling "breakers" are a surfer's dream, but storm waves can seriously damage harbors, seawalls, and seaside homes and farmland.

Equator

Turning up the heat

Satellites equipped with heat-sensitive cameras are used to map the temperature of the oceans. The oceans absorb huge amounts of heat from the Sun. Water temperature is highest near the Equator (shown orange/red) where this heating effect is strongest. Currents then carry the warm water to colder areas (green/blue). Temperature determines what creatures live in the water.

In the **Pacific**, a sea level rise of just 3.3 ft (1 m) could **swamp** hundreds of low-lying **islands**

The tides

As the Moon sweeps around the Earth, the force of its gravity pulls a bulge of water toward it. (Gravity is an invisible force that "tries" to pull two objects toward one another.) The motion of the Earth also creates another bulge at the far side. These bulges cause the tides. Plants and animals that live on seashores depend on the daily rise and fall of the tide.

SUN

When Sun and Moon are in line, their combined pull creates high tides called spring tides.

Moon orbits the Earth.

EARTH

Exaggerated bulge of water caused by the pull of the Moon and Sun.

A seafaring nut

Coconuts are great travelers. They can stand long periods in salt water and can drift up to 2,800 miles (4,500 km) on tropical ocean currents – and still take root when they arrive on a distant beach. The plant probably originated in Polynesia in the Pacific Ocean, but has now spread throughout the tropics, riding the great ocean currents.

Ocean warming could alter **climates** on land and affect crop-growing seasons

This sea arch in England will eventually collapse from the pounding action of the waves.

Wear and tear

Pounding waves break pieces of rock from cliffs and grind them down to pebbles and eventually into fine sand. This arch formed when two wave-worn caves, on opposite sides of the headland, met in the middle. In time, the arch will collapse, leaving a pillar of rock.

Atlantic Ocean
The saltiest of the world's oceans, it also has the highest variation between high and low tides.

Indian Ocean
Rising sea temperatures would threaten coral reefs in the waters near the Equator.

Anchovy

Plankton

Fur seal

Upsetting the balance

Peru's cool coastal waters are rich with plankton (tiny plants and animals) that provide food for fish. Every few years, a current of warm water, called El Niño, kills the plankton and the fish move away. The effect is disastrous because fur seals and seabirds need the fish for their survival.

Antarctic Ocean
Global warming has caused unusually large sections of the Antarctic ice sheet to break off.

Birth of a storm

A hurricane starts when warm, damp air rises over a very warm patch of ocean. As the rising column of air gets bigger, it sucks in more warm air at its base, and starts to rotate. In a fully grown hurricane, the circular walls of cloud can be 12 miles (20 km) high, surrounding a calm "eye" 6–30 miles (10–50 km) across.

Storm brewing
Cloud bands begin to form around an area of low pressure.

Hurricane forming
The cloud walls thicken and the "eye" starts to show.

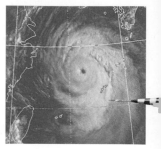

Mature hurricane
The full-grown hurricane moves across the China Sea.

Hurricane Alert

The most violent and destructive storms on Earth begin at sea. Known as hurricanes or cyclones, these revolving storms can be 620 miles (1,000 km) across. They form over warm, tropical seas and get their energy from the heat released when water vapor rises from the ocean and condenses into droplets. When a hurricane runs ashore it starts to weaken and die – but not before its huge store of energy is used up. Winds up to 190 mph (300 kmh), torrential rain, and huge storm waves can severely damage coastal habitats such as coral reefs and mangrove forests.

Transatlantic hitchhikers

Hurricanes can blow migratory birds and flying insects thousands of miles off their usual routes. American birds, such as these yellow-bellied sapsuckers, have been seen as far away as Great Britain.

Big hurricanes contain **more energy** than some countries use in a **year**

Storm surge

Giant storm waves driven by hurricane David crash against the shores of the Caribbean island of Martinique in August 1979. Homes and farmland were devastated. Millions of trees uprooted by winds and storm waves add to existing problems of soil erosion in some of the world's poorest areas.

Radar

Sensors in the nose of the plane

Strengthened wings cope with turbulence

Hurricane hunter

This aircraft has been modified to investigate hurricanes. It carries extra radar above the cockpit and atmospheric sensors in the nose. The crew get a rough ride as they fly through a storm taking measurements.

Hurricane **Mitch** wiped out **70 percent** of agriculture in **Honduras**

The aftermath

Relief workers in Honduras start to tackle the devastation left by hurricane Mitch, which tore across the Caribbean Sea in October 1998. By the time the storm passed, more than 11,000 people were dead, 2.7 million were left homeless, and more than $13 billion of damage had been caused. Mitch was the deadliest hurricane to strike Central America for 200 years.

Shock waves

This destruction on the Alaska coast was caused by a giant wave in 1968. The wave was a tsunami – an enormous surge caused by an earthquake beneath the seabed of the north Pacific. Tsunamis are often called tidal waves, but they have nothing to do with tides.

Trees destroyed by the force of the tsunami.

Water spout

Tornadoes are violently spinning wind systems – a bit like hurricanes, but much narrower. On land, they can wreck houses and throw trucks into the air. At sea they suck up huge amounts of water, creating a dark-gray "pipe" like this.

Phytoplankton
These tiny plants drift near the sea surface. They use the Sun's energy to convert water and carbon dioxide into food.

Zooplankton
The smallest animals in the food chain include the microscopic larvae of crabs, shrimps, and other creatures.

Perfect BALANCE

Plants and animals that live in the sea look very different from those on land. But their ways of life and habitats are similar. Plants within the oceans do the same job as the grasslands and forests on land – they capture the Sun's energy and turn it into food. As on land, these plants provide food for grazing animals, while the grazers, in turn, provide food for the hunters. Marine habitats range from rocky and sandy shores through coral reefs and seaweed forests to the cold, dark depths of ocean basins. Communities of plants and animals have evolved to meet the challenges of each habitat. Disturbing this balance can have far-reaching effects for both animal and human life.

Ocean pastures
This satellite picture has been colored to show the distribution of phytoplankton in the oceans. Red areas have the most, blue the least. These plants provide food for marine animals, and release oxygen into the atmosphere.

First predators
Schools of small fish, such as these anchovies, are the first of a series of predators (animals that prey on other animals).

Airborne predator
Many seabirds, such as this brown pelican, feed almost entirely on small fish.

Food chain
Every living thing needs food to fuel the processes of life – growth, development, and reproduction. A food chain is a line of feeding links between one type of creature and another. In the sunlit zones, phytoplankton grow and multiply. These tiny plants are eaten by animal plankton. Fish, such as anchovies, eat these but are eaten, in turn, by still larger fish. This continues until there is a top predator, such as a shark. A food chain need not be long. Some whales feed directly on plankton.

A drop of seawater can contain millions of phytoplankton

Fish hunters
Larger fish, such as cod, feed on the smaller fish as well as on clams, shrimps, and worms.

Squid fishing off the US coast leaves seals and dolphins short of food

Upsetting the balance

Human activities can have a disastrous effect when they upset the balance of hunters and hunted in the oceans. Fishing for sharks is a popular sport off Tasmania. Sharks feed on octopuses, and removing the sharks causes the number of octopuses to rise. Octopuses then eat more of their natural prey – spiny lobsters – and the balance is changed.

Octopus
The octopus has a powerful beak which makes short work of lobsters, snails, and shellfish.

ADAPTING TO HABITAT

You will need: rubber gloves, 2 types of seaweed, 2 plastic bags, colored tape, kitchen scales, clothespins and line.

Color-code the seaweeds.

Store in a plastic bag.

1 WHEN YOU VISIT A ROCKY BEACH collect two small bunches of seaweed. One of the seaweeds should grow at the water's edge at low tide. The other should be gathered from near the high tide mark.

Weigh out an equal amount of each seaweed.

2 CAREFULLY WEIGH each bunch of seaweed. Remove pieces from the heavier bunch until it weighs exactly the same as the lighter bunch of seaweed.

3 HANG THE bunches out in a dry place. Weigh them daily for four days. The seaweed that grew near the water will lose weight faster than the one that grew higher up the beach.

This shows that: seaweeds that grow higher up the beach – and are out of the sea for most of the day – are better adapted for holding on to vital water.

Large sharks have only one natural enemy – humans

Top predator
This great white shark is at the top of the food chain. It can only be killed by humans, old age, or disease.

MARINE BIOLOGIST
CARL MEYER

CARL MEYER IS BASED AT THE HAWAII INSTITUTE OF MARINE BIOLOGY, WHERE HE STUDIES THE SHARKS THAT THRIVE AROUND HAWAII. TRACKING THE movement of these endangered creatures takes Carl from the waters of Waikiki Marine Reserve to the turbulent Pacific Ocean.

A day in the life of a
MARINE BIOLOGIST

It is necessary to understand how far sharks roam in order to design effective conservation measures.

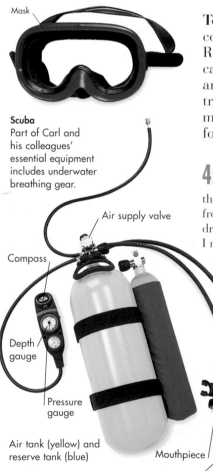

Mask

Scuba
Part of Carl and his colleagues' essential equipment includes underwater breathing gear.

Air supply valve

Compass

Depth gauge

Pressure gauge

Air tank (yellow) and reserve tank (blue)

Mouthpiece

Emergency mouthpiece

Today, Carl and his colleagues from the Shark Research Group plan to capture a large tiger shark and equip it with a sonic transmitter so that its movements can be followed.

4:00pm I collect 30 large tuna heads (bait for the evening's shark fishing trip) from a local fish market and drive to Honolulu harbor, where I meet up with colleagues Aaron and Steve. We load the bait, fishing gear, and diving and computer equipment onto our research vessel.

5:00pm First we have to double-check the boat engine and electrical systems, and radio for permission to depart. Then we leave the harbor and make the 1.25-mile (2-km) trip out to our shark fishing grounds.

5:30pm On reaching our destination we bait and place three shark longlines in 65–325 ft (20–100 m) of water. Each longline consists of ten large steel hooks, attached to a main rope line by biteproof stainless-steel cable. Longlines are anchored on the seabed and their positions are marked with surface floats. When the last line has been set we return to harbor hoping that the bloody fish heads will attract sharks during the night.

> ❝ Calmness, patience, and intense concentration are required when working with large tiger sharks. ❞

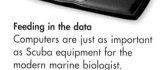

Feeding in the data
Computers are just as important as Scuba equipment for the modern marine biologist.

6:30am We leave at dawn the next morning, full of anticipation, to retrieve the longlines. Powerful jerks on the first line indicate that something large has taken the bait during the night. As we stare into the dark-blue water, a huge, green-brown shape with massive, blunt head and gigantic girth, looms suddenly out of the depths. It has the unmistakable profile of a 16 ft (5 m) tiger shark – luck is on our side!

A sharp dive knife is carried in a sheath.

Shark inspection
A juvenile tiger shark is closely inspected prior to release. The tiger stripes – from which this animal gets its name – are clearly visible on the flanks of this young shark.

8:00am We attempt to secure the shark alongside our 20 ft (6 m) Boston Whaler by using the hook cable and a noose around the shark's tail. As we maneuver the tail rope into position, the powerful shark struggles violently and it takes several attempts to slide the noose over the thrashing tail. We fight hard to roll the shark upside down and place it in a trancelike state known as "tonic immobility." After measuring the now docile shark, I use a sharp knife to pierce a small hole in the tough skin alongside the shark's dorsal

Back in the sea
Tiger sharks are carefully measured and tagged with a numbered identification tag before they are released.

fin and insert an identification tag beneath the skin. The numbered tag will allow this shark to be recognized if it is ever captured again.

8:30am Next I have to implant an 8-in (20-cm) long transmitter into the shark's gut cavity. I use a large scalpel to make a 6-in (15-cm) incision through the thick skin and muscle of the shark's belly wall. I insert the transmitter, stitch the incision closed, and remove the hook and tail rope. We turn the shark over and release it, watching it swim effortlessly away. The transmitter will gather data about the shark's movements through the ocean and send the information to special receivers anchored on the seabed.

9:30am We put on our Scuba gear, retrieve a receiver from the seabed, and download the stored data to a laptop computer.

Special equipment
The transmitter (far left) is implanted in the shark's gut cavity. The other transmitter may be attached externally to a shark's skin.

10:30am We return to harbor, wash and stow away the equipment, and head to the lab to analyze our data. The information we have collected on tiger sharks has already been used to dissuade the Hawaii state government from indiscriminately killing hundreds of sharks in response to shark attacks on people.

Up from the seabed
A bottom monitor, retrieved from the seabed, is washed down with fresh water before data from transmitter-equipped sharks is downloaded to a laptop.

PACIFIC OCEAN

H A W A I I

OAHU

• Honolulu

MOLOKAI

• Track started
○ Track ended

Tiger shark routes
This map shows the tracks (colored lines) of transmitter-carrying sharks off the south coast of Oahu.

Bowhead whale
8,000 remaining

Hector's dolphin
3,000–6,000 remaining

Blue whale
5,800 remaining

Finless porpoise
Numbers unknown

Whale watch

With their fast boats and exploding harpoons, whalers almost wiped out some of the great whales between 1850 and 1950. Although most whaling has now stopped, whales and their smaller cousins, the dolphins and porpoises, are still at risk. Chemical pollution affects species that live in enclosed seas, such as the Baltic and Mediterranean, as well as the whales that migrate along coastlines. Military exercises using depth charges also scare whales away from traditional feeding and breeding areas. But there is hope for these giants of the sea. In the early 1900s, there were only a few California gray whales. Since the species was protected in 1946, however, the population has increased to a healthy 8,000 whales.

> "Threats such as climate change and ozone depletion are becoming just as deadly as the harpoon"
>
> THE ENVIRONMENTAL INVESTIGATION AGENCY

Factory ship
A minke whale is hauled up the ramp of a Japanese factory ship in the Antarctic Ocean. In 1994 the International Whaling Commission declared this ocean a whale sanctuary, but Japanese whalers still hunt whales there in the name of scientific research.

Voices of protest
Many people believe that whaling should be banned completely. Others think that endangered species should be protected, but that other more numerous species, such as minke whales, could be hunted if the numbers caught were limited.

Fin whale
46,000 remaining

Vaquita
Less than 500 remaining

Endangered whales and dolphins

Of the world's 79 species of whales, dolphins, and porpoises, two are now so endangered that they could disappear forever in the next 10 years. Fifteen more could become extinct within a human lifetime.

Deep-sea fishing

fleets **rob** some species of whale of their natural **food supplies**

ACTION!
SAVE WHALES

Support organizations that are fighting to end whaling.

Always buy "dolphin safe" fish. Millions of dolphins die in nets used by tuna fishers.

Some **airlines** refuse to carry **dolphins** destined for marine parks and **aquariums**

Safari at sea

The sight of a whale's tail fins rising out of the water is a treat for whale watchers. Tourists can take boat safaris to see whales from places like San Diego on the California coast. This kind of ecotourism does little harm as long as the boats go out in small groups and do not chase the whales. In fact, whales often swim closer for a good look at their visitors!

Pleasure boats

kill and injure **hundreds of** small whales **each year**

CHUKCHI SEA

NORTH AMERICA

ASIA

BERING SEA

Most whales give birth to single calves.

The calf is born at the breeding grounds a year after mating takes place.

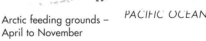

Arctic feeding grounds – April to November

Breeding grounds – December to April

PACIFIC OCEAN

MEXICO

Migration routes

Every year, gray whales make a 10,000-mile (16,000-km) round trip. They swim between their feeding grounds in the cold northern seas and the warm Gulf of California, where they give birth to their young. A few also swim between Russia and South Korea.

Baja Peninsula

Is it right?

Dolphins are very intelligent and seem to enjoy performing. However, dolphinarium pools are tiny compared with the open sea, and captive whales are never as healthy as wild ones. Some countries are phasing out these shows and returning captive whales to their natural habitats.

No fish in the *sea*

I**n some areas, fish** such as cod and haddock have almost disappeared, and some of the world's richest fishing grounds are in trouble. The main cause of the problem is overfishing. Just 50 years ago, the total world fish catch was about 14 million tons a year. By 1989, this had soared to 73 million, and things have gone wrong since then. Technology – echosounders that pinpoint schools of fish and nets big enough to swallow jumbo jets – enables today's factory trawlers to catch, process, and freeze hundreds of tons of fish a day.

Fishing in Sri Lanka

Traditional fisheries that use baited lines (as shown here), nets, or small boats account for almost half the fish eaten today. There is no waste – all the fish are used as food. In contrast, most of the fish caught by factory trawlers are used to make animal feed.

Great American Fish Count

Divers around the American coasts are helping conservationists. They collect information on the types of fish they see, and how many fish there are. First, volunteers are taught to identify local species. During each dive they keep records using special underwater writing slates. Later, they send in the details to the project headquarters.

> **"The world catch is in decline and is expected to continue to decline..."**

DR. MERYL WILLIAMS
DIRECTOR, INTERNATIONAL CENTER
FOR LIVING AQUATIC RESOURCES

Harvesting the sea

Trawl nets are funnel-shaped, with a wide opening and a narrow tail, or "cod end." The cod end is where the fish collect as the net is towed through the water. An average-size net like this will hold about a ton of fish. The huge nets used by supertrawlers can scoop up to 100 tons at a time.

The highly valued **bluefin tuna** has been **fished** almost to **extinction**

Major fishing regions of the world

On the map shown right each fish represents one million tons of fish caught in one year. The richest fishing grounds are on continental shelves, where the water is less than 650 ft (200 m) deep. They are also found in coastal areas where cold water, rich in food, wells up from the depths. This is where herring, anchovies, cod, haddock, mackerel, and bass are found.

Icelandic herring
Strict controls have saved the herring from being wiped out in some areas.

Caribbean
Overfishing threatens red snapper, tuna, and many shark species.

ASIA

EUROPE

AFRICA

NORTH AMERICA

SOUTH AMERICA

AUSTRALIA

Pacific northwest
Russia, Korea, China, Japan, and America all fish the northwest Pacific with big factory trawlers.

Peruvian fishery
In 25 years, anchoveta hauls fell from 13 million tons a year to just over 5 million.

Some **trawlers** throw back 40 percent of their **catch** – **dead** and wasted

The electronic tag stores information. It is collected when the fish is caught.

Plaice tagging

This tag records information about a fish's movements between its summer feeding grounds and its winter spawning (egg-laying) grounds. Understanding fish behavior is important to help avoid overfishing.

Dolphins in danger

Every year, thousands of dolphins drown after they become trapped in drift nets. These long nets are suspended from floats, and hang down in the water like invisible curtains. This striped dolphin is part of the unwanted haul that fishermen call "by-catch." Good management of fisheries is helping to reduce by-catch in many parts of the world.

FISHERIES OFFICER
KEITH SAUNDERS

KEITH SAUNDERS IS BASED IN BROOME, WESTERN AUSTRALIA. HIS JOB IS TO PATROL THE SEAS LOOKING FOR BOATS THAT MIGHT BE FISHING ILLEGALLY. The area of ocean he covers is vast – stretching from the Timor Sea in the north to Australia's islands in Antarctica in the south. He is also an official Marine Park Ranger.

A day in the life of a
FISHERIES PROTECTION OFFICER

Fishing must be regulated to preserve fish stocks and to conserve the numbers of endangered species

Identification badge
Whenever I board a foreign fishing vessel, I introduce myself to the captain and show my identification badge.

Today, I am on duty at my office in Broome. My work is unpredictable and I can be called out to sea day or night. Our boat – the Royal Australian Navy *HMAS Geraldton* – is alongside the jetty, ready to put to sea at any time.

5:00pm I receive a radio signal telling me that two foreign fishing boats have been spotted in Australian

Tuna
One of the largest fish to be caught commercially.

waters to the north. I collect my patrol gear and prepare to leave. My kit contains everything I need to operate at sea and to board foreign fishing vessels in all but the most extreme weather conditions.

7:00pm We set sail on the *HMAS Geraldton* and are guided to the fishing boats by coded radio signals from surveillance aircraft. We plot our route – the journey will take us a full 12 hours. This gives me plenty of time to brief the navy crew about what we will do and how to board the fishing vessels safely.

HMAS Geraldton
Our patrol boat is capable of cruising at speeds of more than 25 knots.

7:00am We reach the two boats. I board the first vessel from a Rigid Hull Inflatable Boat (RHIB) carried on board the *Geraldton* and speak to the fishers in Indonesian. They tell me that they have not been fishing in Australian waters but are on their way to Browse Island, which lies 30 miles (45 km) to the southeast. Indonesian boats are allowed to fish in an area that includes Browse Island through an agreement between the Australian and Indonesian governments called the Memorandum of Understanding (MOU).

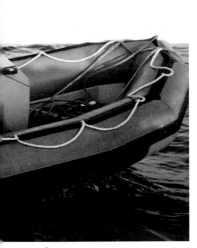

Boarding party
The Rigid Hull Inflatable Boat is lowered from the stern deck of *HMAS Geraldton* to carry a boarding party.

After explaining the rules of fishing within the MOU area, I give the fisher the course to the island and wish him *selemat tinggal* (goodbye). He bids me *selemat jalan* (goodbye too). We set sail for Browse Island ourselves. The island is an important nesting area for green turtles, which are protected by international law. The turtles' eggs are a popular food in Asia, and we need to check that they are not being collected illegally.

9:30am We arrive at Browse Island and go ashore to check the beaches for turtle activity. It has been a busy night and at least 50 turtles have come ashore to lay their eggs in the sand. Two of the nests have been dug up and their eggs removed – they are surrounded by human footprints that lead down to the sea. We check the fishing boats in the area but find no sign of the eggs, so we head north for Ashmore reef.

4:00pm Arrive at Ashmore, where I spend the afternoon patrolling the outer shallow reefs. As a Marine Park Ranger, I help manage the National Park, which is home to many threatened species and fragile ecosystems. Animals, such as the trochus and sea cucumber that live in the sands and reefs of Ashmore, are targets for illegal fishers. Tons of the animals may be taken at a time, regardless of their size. Because trochus and sea cucumbers take years to grow, it is easy to wipe out whole populations very quickly by overfishing. Although we can reduce the damage by chasing and prosecuting illegal

Keeping a lookout
Fisheries officers scour the vast expanses of ocean in aircraft like this Customs Coastwatch turboprop as well as in high-speed patrol boats.

Vessel inspection
On board a fishing vessel, we check that fish are not being taken illegally. We measure the size of the fish and ensure that bag limits (how many fish can be taken in one day) are not being ignored.

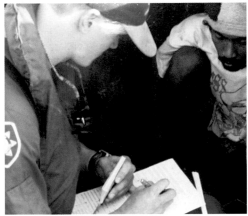

fishers, we know that they will return. It is our job to teach them that their activities are harmful because they will eventually wipe out the very species that they come to catch.

8:00pm We receive an urgent signal from Canberra. A Coastwatch patrol aircraft has detected an illegal vessel 100 miles (160 km) to the southeast of us outside the MOU area. We head off at full speed, setting a course to intercept them five hours later.

1:30am We board the boat and unfortunately find several tons of trochus shell on board. The captain agrees he has broken the law, and his vessel, with its crew of 23, is towed back to Broome.

Back at Broome I will investigate the case and, if required, I will prosecute the captain and crew under the Australian Fisheries Management Act. If found guilty, the captain can lose the boat and will have to pay a large fine. However, we are working with the local fishers and trying to help them understand the need to protect the different species that live in the world's oceans.

> **Only with the help of fishers can we protect the biological diversity of the sea.**

Fishing area
Within the MOU zone, only traditional fishing – without help from mechanical equipment – is allowed.

Green turtles
Browse Island is a key breeding site for green turtles.

Trochus
The trochus is sought after for jewelry, buttons, and ornaments.

Sea cucumber
The sea cucumber, or trepang, is eaten as a delicacy in Asia.

Trochus buttons

EXPLOITING *the* SEA

T he oceans have always provided people with food. Today, there are other important industries that rely on raw materials from the sea. Oil and gas are extracted from rocks beneath the ocean floor, and tin and titanium are dredged from coastal sandbars. Certain seaweeds are gathered and used in processed foods, while seawater itself is treated to make clean drinking water as well as salt. The deep ocean floors are littered with fist-sized nodules rich in manganese, copper, and nickel. They are not exploited yet – but they could prove important mineral resources of the future.

Fish farming

In many countries, fish are raised in wire-mesh pens. Although fish farming reduces the numbers of fish caught in the wild, it does have problems. Here, fish food has caused a blanket of algae to grow near the pens. This algae can choke natural life nearby.

SHELL / ESSO
AUK-A

Energy from the sea

Almost a quarter of the oil and gas we use comes from beneath the shallow seas of the continental shelves. The oil and gas are extracted by drilling down through the rocks from huge platforms, such as this one in the North Sea. Oil platform workers check constantly for leaks and spills that could harm the environment.

Seaweed farming

Cultivating seaweed is a major industry in parts of Asia. In Japan, people eat more seaweed than anywhere else in the world. It is cultivated in shallow coastal seas. In the Philippines, seaweeds are used to make carrageenan. This is a thickening and binding agent used in sausages, yogurt, shampoos, cosmetics, and toothpastes.

Drugs that could help fight cancer have been extracted from sponges

Salt from the sea

A worker in Thailand rakes sea salt into piles. Extracting the salt is a slow business. Seawater is channeled through a series of shallow ponds where sunshine and wind evaporate the water. This makes the brine (salty water) more and more concentrated. After 18 months, the bed of the final pond is covered in a layer of glistening white salt crystals.

Fish farms around the world provide us with more than 4 million tons of fish a year

For safety, waste gas is burned off at the end of a long boom.

Fresh water

Around the world, about 13,000 desalination (de-salting) plants produce fresh water from salt water. Desalination plants are expensive, but in desert areas they are often the only solution to water shortages. This installation in Dubai is one of 35 big plants in the United Arab Emirates.

HOW SALTY IS THE SEA?

You will need: greaseproof paper, baking tray, plastic bottle, seawater, magnifying glass.

Seawater collected during a trip to the beach.

EXPERIMENT

1 LINE THE BAKING TRAY with greaseproof paper. Press the paper firmly down into the corners and turn it up at the edges so that it can hold water.

2 POUR IN ABOUT 1 pint (half a liter) of seawater. Leave the tray in a warm place, such as a cabinet or on a sunny window ledge.

3 WHEN ALL THE WATER has evaporated, examine the dried salt crystals under a magnifying glass. Most of the crystals will be cube-shaped.

This shows that: the sea is full of salt minerals. Most of this is the same chemical as table salt.

CORAL REEFS

AND COASTLINES

> 66 Corals do not appear to be able to adapt fast enough to keep pace with changes in ocean temperature. 99
>
> **PROFESSOR OVE HOEGH-GULDBERG**
> **UNIVERSITY OF SYDNEY, AUSTRALIA**

CORAL REEFS, BEACHES, SALT MARSHES, AND MANGROVE SWAMPS ARE COMPLEX PLACES DELICATELY balanced between the sea and the land. They are vital to the planet's well-being, but also very fragile – vulnerable to storm damage, overfishing, pollution, and tourists, as well as environmental changes.

Kayangel (main picture) is a typical atoll in the western Pacific. A ring of coral reefs, just below sea level, encloses a lagoon, while sand has piled up on parts of the reef to create small islands. Even a 3.3 ft (1 m) rise in sea level would cover hundreds of atolls like this. The inset picture shows a Red Sea coral reef damaged by tourists taking souvenirs.

Reef in DANGER

Two-thirds of reefs in the Caribbean are threatened by overharvesting and pollution

Coral reefs are the richest habitats in the ocean. Just a few miles of reef can contain well over 3,000 species – from minute shrimps to fish weighing more than half a ton. A reef is a massive, rocky structure, but it is also surprisingly fragile. The tiny animals called polyps which build the reef can only thrive when conditions are just right. The water must be shallow enough for sunlight to reach the coral, and the water should be at least 65°F (18°C) warm. It must also be free from mud and pollution. Any change in these conditions puts the reef at risk.

The living reef

A coral reef swarms with life. With all its nooks and crannies it provides a home for hundreds of different types of marine plants and animals as well as the living corals themselves. The reef is a complete ecosystem in its own right – a complex world where scavengers, filter-feeders, plant-eaters, and hunters all depend on one another for survival.

Tentacles are armed with stinging cells.

There is just one body opening.

Each polyp makes its own skeleton cup.

Only the surface of the reef is alive.

Reef builders

A reef is built from the piled-up skeletons of tiny animals called polyps. Each polyp makes a hard limestone cup to live in – poking out its tentacles to feed, and pulling back inside when danger comes along. When the polyps die, their skeletons remain. These gradually build up to create a coral reef.

The reef builds up layer by layer.

Brain coral

Organ-pipe coral

Staghorn coral

Bleached coral

These scientists are studying bleached corals in Polynesia, in the Pacific Ocean. Corals get some of their color from tiny algae that live inside them. If the water temperature rises, or the reef is polluted, the algae leave and the coral turns white. If the right conditions do not return quickly, the reef will die.

Anchor damage

Reefs suffer a great deal of damage when tourist boats lower anchors and chains to the seafloor (shown here). Although the old limestone rock at the heart of a reef is tough enough to rip the bottom out of a ship, the thin layer of living coral on the surface of the reef is delicate.

A market for coral

Corals grow in a range of appealing shapes and colors, and thousands of tons are sold every year to tourists. This Bali islander is collecting a basket of dead coral to sell. Each time a lump of coral is sold, another piece is hacked off a reef to take its place on the market stall. It can take decades for the coral to regrow.

> "Pollution, overfishing, and overuse have put many of our unique reefs at risk..."
>
> BILL CLINTON
> US PRESIDENT (1993–2001)

Some of the world's coral reefs may be 2.5 million years old

Mining reefs for building materials continues in the Indian Ocean

ACTION!
SAVE THE REEF

If you are diving or snorkeling on a reef, look – but never touch.

Do not buy souvenirs made of coral, rare shells, or parts of other reef creatures.

Island REFUGE

When British naturalist Charles Darwin visited the Galápagos Islands in 1835, he discovered giant tortoises, iguanas that fed on seaweed, and cormorants that could not fly. Darwin soon realized that each species had adapted to the special set of conditions on its island home. This discovery led him to his theory of evolution. Islands are still home to unusual species, but many have been wiped out by cats and rats introduced from visiting ships. People have also destroyed habitats in their search for timber and minerals or by taking land for farming.

Island giant
At 10 ft (3 m) long and 300 lb (136 kg) in weight, the Komodo dragon is the world's largest lizard. It lives on Komodo Island in Indonesia, and eats deer, bush pigs, eggs, and carrion. Hunters almost wiped out the dragon, but the 5,000 that remain are now protected by law.

Animals **brought** to islands by people **cause 70** percent of **extinctions of native** species

Birth of an island
In 1963, a volcano erupted 425 ft (130 m) down on the floor of the Atlantic Ocean off the coast of Iceland. Gradually, ash and lava built up higher and higher until the tip of the volcano burst through the surface of the water. A new island – Surtsey – was born. Two years later, wind-blown seeds had taken root and the first insects and birds had arrived.

By 1990, there were 20 different plant species growing on Surtsey.

Once plants were established, birds began to nest on the island.

ACTION!
ISLAND RESCUE

Support local and international conservation organizations that help protect island habitats.

When visiting islands, respect the local wildlife.

Crazy ants
These ants get their name from their habit of dashing around in constant frantic activity.

Ant attack

In 1998, scientists discovered that crazy ants – a species accidentally introduced to Bird Island in the Seychelles – had become a serious problem. They had infested the nests of sooty terns and driven away 60,000 breeding pairs of these birds. Now, ant control measures are being planned.

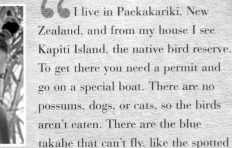

Birds in...
Kaka numbers on Kapiti Island have grown after the removal of alien species.

Kaka

Aliens out
Alien species removed from Kapiti included 22,500 possums.

Possum

" I live in Paekakariki, New Zealand, and from my house I see Kapiti Island, the native bird reserve. To get there you need a permit and go on a special boat. There are no possums, dogs, or cats, so the birds aren't eaten. There are the blue takahe that can't fly, like the spotted kiwi. You don't see this kiwi in the day, though, because it sleeps then. The kaka sit on your head and eat from your hand. The birds eat the berries from the native trees, and the insects. You are allowed to take only photos and leave only footprints! "

Rehua Watson.

Habitat destruction

Christmas Island in the Indian Ocean has been devastated by phosphate mining. To get at the deposits, miners have to cut down the dense rain forest cover, and then dig out the phosphate. This leaves a desolate landscape of bare limestone rock. The destruction has endangered several rare seabirds that nest in the tall trees, and also several land birds.

Cash clearance

This banana plantation on the Caribbean island of Martinique shows a problem common to many tropical islands. Most of the original vegetation has been cleared to make room for crops that local farmers can sell to developed countries. This robs native birds, mammals, and insects of their natural habitats and food supplies.

Takahe

Kapiti nature reserve

Kapiti Island, about 3 miles (5 km) off the southwestern tip of North Island, New Zealand, has been made into a bird sanctuary. It was a huge task that took several years. To make the island safe for rare native birds such as the kaka and takahe, thousands of non-native predators, including possums, cats, weasels, and rats, were removed. Habitat-destroying domestic animals, like goats, sheep, and cattle, were also removed.

MARINE BIOLOGIST
AMANDA VINCENT

DR. AMANDA VINCENT IS CO-DIRECTOR OF PROJECT SEAHORSE, AN INTERNATIONAL GROUP OF BIOLOGISTS AND SOCIAL WORKERS WHO ARE TRYING TO SECURE a safe future for seahorses and their habitats. She works with a Filipino team on a community project based in the traditional fishing village of Handumon.

A day in the life of a
SEAHORSE SPECIALIST

Project Seahorse is committed to conserving seahorses and their habitats while respecting human needs.

Today, I'm in Handumon in the central Philippines. I plan to go looking for seahorses with the local fishers. It is a world away from my life in Montreal, Canada, where I teach at McGill University.

Lighting the way
A seahorse fisher lights the lantern that will help him to spot seahorses in the still-dark hours of early morning.

1:00am A seahorse fisher calls through the bamboo walls of our staff house to see if I'm awake. He then waits as I struggle into my wetsuit. We make our way out through the mangroves and into his small outrigger boat. He lights the lantern and starts paddling toward the dim outline that is Mahanay Island.

2:30am The fisher and I slide into the water. We position ourselves on either side of the bow under the lantern and swim slowly ahead, scanning the bottom for fish and crabs. He spears anything that he thinks he can sell later, twisting seahorses off their perches before popping them into a small container on the boat.

5:00am Our swimming has slowed greatly. The fisher and I are both feeling despondent. Years of overfishing means there really isn't much to catch, or many seahorses left to spot. The dawn comes up slowly and we clamber into the boat,

cold and tired. The fisher will sell the seahorses to buyers in the village. From there, live ones will be sold to aquarium collectors, while dead ones will be sold as ornaments. They are also used as ingredients for traditional Chinese medicines (seahorses are believed to cure illnesses such as asthma). The demand for seahorses is great. Worldwide, tens of millions are

Taking measurements
Before you can measure a seahorse, you have to coax it to straighten its tail. The size of the seahorses is noted while the colored tag tells us their age.

caught every year, which has caused their numbers to fall in many areas. Relatively little is known about the biology of seahorses, and part of my work here is to study how their populations respond to fishing.

6:00am We arrive home at Handumon and head up to the staff house. The team biologists and village

Studying the catch
Fishers bring their catch of seahorses to the staff house every day. Here, Marivic and I are sorting and measuring them.

Positioning a seahorse cage
Unusually, it is male seahorses who carry their young. The males are protected in a cage until they give birth.

Fair craft
The team's community adviser, Mia, displays crafts that earn extra income for seahorse fishing families.

trainees measure, weigh, and document the seahorses the fisher caught. These few animals will earn half his pay for that night. Another important part of our work here is to build the support of the local people. If we are to succeed in protecting the seahorses and their habitats, it's no good just telling the fishers to stop taking the animals, because seahorses are their livelihood.

6:30am More fishers arrive. We grab hot drinks and sit talking on the balcony. The hot topic for discussion is poaching. The village has set up an 82-acre (33-hectare) marine sanctuary where no fishing of any kind is permitted. There is an adjacent zone where only fishing with traditional methods is allowed. Both are patrolled by the villagers, but poachers still strike, attracted by the larger catches in these areas.

Seahorse seas
The tiny village of Handumon lies just to the west of Talibon on the island of Bohol in the Philippines.

8:30am Breakfast at last – rice and fish as usual. Our high school apprentices arrive. They work with us every weekend, helping with our conservation projects in exchange for scholarships that allow them to continue in school. Today, our community organizer, Mia, is helping them develop a puppet show to teach young children about environmental issues. I work with them a bit, making them laugh at my mistakes in the local Cebuano language.

Male seahorse
This adult, big-bellied seahorse can inflate his pouch to attract females during courtship.

10:30am Jonathan, the lead biologist, and I go to look at the seahorses in a protected study site beyond the next island. The village assistant helps us load our outrigger boat, Project Seahorse, with dive gear, food, and water. Then he steers us out through the nearby mangrove plantation.

11:00am We plunge into the water and start looking for seahorses that we have previously fitted with tags. They are difficult to spot, but we eventually find most of them. We note the tag number on their collars, their location, their reproductive state, and their behavior. It is slow and careful work, and we only pause to eat.

“Our vision is a world where populations of seahorses are secure.”

New generation
This newborn seahorse is 0.03 in (8 mm) long. Seahorses hang on to algae and corals with their tails.

5:00pm We arrive home, wash the gear, then start entering the new data in our computers. We have no permanent electricity supply at Handumon, so we hope that our solar power will last until we have finished. The team leader, Marivic, reviews the day over supper.

7:00pm We plan for a meeting with the municipal officials tomorrow. We will ask them to give more support to the villagers who are trying so hard to manage their marine resources wisely. I desperately need sleep but must complete my reports before I can rest.

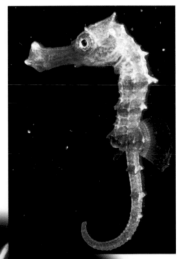

COASTAL *Care*

At the boundary between land and sea, the coasts provide a huge variety of habitats for some of the most fascinating animals and plants on our planet. But coasts also attract people in vast numbers – many come on vacation, others to find permanent homes. This increases the level of development and pollution in these areas. However, worldwide beach cleanup events are helping to preserve the world's coastlines. The projects help people to understand the problems and enable them to do something positive.

Cliff tops
Short grasses grow in the thin soil. Puffins and Manx shearwaters nest in cliff-top burrows.

Rock pools
Home to crabs, limpets, anemones, and starfish, the rock pools are filled with many seaweeds.

Sandy beach
Hundreds of species of worms and shellfish live hidden in their burrows beneath the sand.

Rocky headlands
Birds such as kittiwakes, guillemots, and razorbills nest on narrow cliff ledges.

Survival techniques

The coast is a harsh place for living things. Seaside plants must cope with salt spray, and survive on shifting sands or tiny amounts of soil in rock crevices. Many have short stems and cushionlike leaves to protect them from the buffeting and drying effect of the wind. To avoid the sun and marauding seabirds, worms, and cockles burrow into the sand when the tide goes out, while limpets clamp themselves to the rocks and crabs hide under fronds of damp seaweed.

Marram dunes

The shifting surface of a sand dune is a difficult place for any plant to take root. However, marram grass grows quickly and has roots that spread sideways as well as down. This helps to anchor the sand and allows other plants to get established.

Dense roots bind loose sand grains together.

I live in New Jersey, right near Atlantic City. The beach here has changed a lot over the years. When my parents were kids it was clean, but now the water pollution is so bad that fish often wash up dead. If you walk along the beach, you find broken bottles, plastic cups, and even cigarette butts. Because I care about the beach, I do voluntary work with a group called Clean Ocean Action who try to protect the ocean. This makes the beach a better place for the animals that live there – and for the people, too.

Jenna Gatto

ACTION!
BE GREEN

Always take your litter home with you.

Cut through plastic six-pack yokes before throwing them away.

Take part in a local beach-cleaning project.

Beach cleanup

In many countries, young people take part in beach cleanup operations. The detailed surveys carried out during these events show what the main types of garbage are and where they come from. This helps governments make better enviromental laws.

Lethal litter

Of all the litter that people leave on beaches, the most dangerous are plastic bags and yokes that hold beverage cans. Birds and seals get their heads or legs caught in them. This can lead to them drowning or being strangled.

This American coot is caught in the plastic loops of a six-pack yoke.

Seabird sanctuary

The eggs and nestlings of some species, like these little terns, are often well camouflaged. This means they are almost impossible to see against a background of pebbles – until it's too late. Look out for notices that ask you to keep off beaches where birds are breeding.

Chemical beach

Occasionally a metal drum, or a plastic container of liquid or powder, may wash up on a beach. It could contain acid or poisonous chemicals – and might even be giving off dangerous fumes. This is no ordinary beach trash and should not be approached. Tell a parent or teacher.

TOURIST TRAFFIC

Within ten years more than a billion people will be taking their annual vacations overseas. Many countries – especially those with beautiful beaches and coral reefs – depend on tourists to provide a living income for their people. But tourism brings problems, too. Building airports, roads, and hotels, providing enough fresh water, and disposing of sewage all have an effect on coastal environments. Also, the sheer numbers of visitors can threaten local habitats and wildlife. Tourism is important, and here to stay, but it needs to be very carefully planned. Responsible "ecotourism" may help to reduce visitors' impact on the environment.

The human tide

Bournemouth beach, in southern England, is packed with tourists in summer – up to 100,000 of them on 7 miles (11 km) of sandy beach. Every morning and evening a team of 25 workers with hand rakes and tractor-powered machines cleans the entire beach, shifting up to 20 tons of flotsam and litter a day. This cleanup costs huge amounts of money.

Scarce water

Goa, on the west coast of India, is a tourist paradise with long sandy beaches fringed with palm trees. But here, and in many other tropical resorts, there's a price to pay. Big hotels with lush gardens are often allowed to take a huge share of scarce fresh water resources, leaving little for the local people.

A big **hotel** uses as much **electricity** as 3,500 medium-sized **households**

Dangerous sports

Waterskiing, powerboating, and jetskiing are great fun, but they can also endanger wildlife. In some vacation resorts they are restricted to certain zones to keep them away from colonies of seals, otters, dolphins, and diving birds, such as cormorants and pelicans.

"The rapid growth of tourism around the Mediterranean Sea is a major threat to the environment and biodiversity of the area."

UNITED NATIONS
ENVIRONMENT PROGRAM
EARTHSCAN 2000

All visitors to **Belize** are charged a **fee** to pay for **nature** conservation in the **country**

Sea urchin

Starfish

Sea sponge

Beware what you buy

Beautiful shells are for sale on this beach in South Africa. If the vendor only collects empty shells for sale, no harm is done. In many parts of the world, however, unscrupulous dealers hunt living shellfish, sea turtles, and rare species of starfish, sea urchins, and sponges. If in doubt, do not buy. You could be breaking international laws.

Endangered species

This green sea turtle has hatched on a tropical beach, and must dash to the sea past marauding seabirds. Even then it is not safe. Hunters kill adult turtles for meat and shells. Also, when adult females come ashore to lay their eggs, there are more dangers from illegal egg collectors, and thoughtless tourists who trespass on protected beaches.

ACTION!
BE RESPECTFUL

Dispose of your litter carefully after a day at the beach.

Don't be tempted to pick plants or flowers that are growing wild.

Stay on marked paths and keep your distance from wildlife.

MARINE MAMMAL MEDIC
KIERAN COPELAND

KIERAN COPELAND WORKS AT THE SOS SEAL RESCUE HOSPITAL BASED AT HUNSTANTON IN ENGLAND. THROUGHOUT THE YEAR, THE HOSPITAL CARES FOR sick or abandoned seals, as well as porpoises and, occasionally, whales. The aim of the hospital is to rehabilitate the seals before releasing them back into the wild.

Seal colony, North Sea
Pups are released as close as possible to where they were rescued – usually near a wild colony such as this.

A day in the life of a
MARINE MAMMAL MEDIC

By understanding more about the behavior of seals, we are better prepared to help with their long-term conservation.

Today, Kieran and his colleagues face a routine day of health checks and feeding. They never know, however, when they may get a call to go out and rescue a seal or seal pup from a nearby beach.

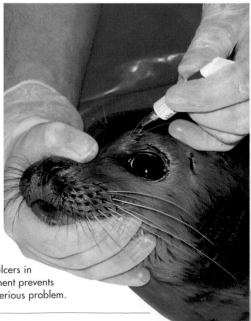

Hunstanton
Common and gray seals live in wild colonies along the North Sea coast.

12:00am Midnight and my shift starts. When I arrive at the Sea Life Aquarium, I feed the latest seal pup casualties in the hospital here. Seal pups are taken in for a variety of reasons. They may have been abandoned by their mothers, damaged by fishing nets, or are sick. We have three pups at the moment, and they need to be fed every four hours. Feeding is a tricky business as I have to insert a tube down one pup's throat so I can pour in a fatty milk substitute. The pup is still too young to take solid food. The other pups have learned to feed for themselves, so I toss them a fish and let them get on with it.

4:00am Same procedure as at midnight with the whole process taking about 30 minutes. The pups in the hospital have to progress through a number of stages of rehabilitation before they are ready for release. If unweaned, they start off on force-fed milk

substitute and then fish until they are able to eat for themselves. Next they will be introduced to our resident seals and will learn to compete for their food. The pups need to weigh at least 77 lb (35 kg) before we can release them back in the sea. Depending on their injuries, it can take 3–6 months before the pup is fit.

Teeth check
Despite their endearing image, seal pups have strong teeth.

Eye check
Seals may arrive with ulcers in their eyes. Quick treatment prevents what could become a serious problem.

8:00am I am first to arrive and open up. I check the pups have not deteriorated before feeding them again. My assistant Barney arrives and prepares the aquarium for opening to the public at 10am. As well as the seals, the aquarium has more than 30 displays, mainly focusing on British marine life.

There's a lot to clean and check. I prepare the treatment schedules for the day and go to treat one of the seals that has an eye infection. The seals' temperatures are also taken, and several other checks completed. Barney and I then grab some breakfast while chatting about how the pups are progressing and our plans for the rest of the day.

10:30am Time for the daily environmental enrichment activities for the resident seals. These are common seals that, for many reasons, would not survive if they were released back into the wild. Fish pulls, ice blocks, and seaweed are designed to make the animals search out and work for their fish. The seals seem to enjoy the exercise and visitors love watching them racing and splashing around.

Feeding time
Once they have learned to eat for themselves, seal pups enjoy regular meals of herring or mackerel.

12:00pm Time to feed the pups again. They have ravenous appetites at this age and get through 6.6 lb (3 kg) of herring a day. The aquarium rescues on average 25 pups every year. They're mostly common pups but we do get the occasional gray seal in the winter.

Injured seal pup
It is important to approach the seal pup with care as it will be scared.

12:30pm A phone call comes through from a member of the public to report an injured pup washed up on a beach. I ask the caller a number of questions to ascertain the exact location of the pup. I also ask about its condition. The pup sounds in poor health so I tell the caller not to touch the pup, but to keep people away and wait until I get there. I load the pup rescue equipment into the van and head off toward Weybourne, which is about an hour away.

1:30pm When I arrive, I find a one-month-old female gray seal pup with a suspected parasite infestation and a dog bite on her back. Although they have the image of being cute and docile, seal pups have quite a nasty bite and can carry viruses that are transferable to humans. I carefully load the pup into a carrying cage and put her into the van. Once back, I let the pup rest for a while after her traumatic journey.

Our best years are the quiet ones as this means there have been fewer seals injured or abandoned.

4:30pm Time to check the pup into our hospital. First I take her temperature and then spray antiseptic onto the wounds. This temporarily turns the skin a strange, green color. The pup is weighed with the assistance of Barney and then we monitor her breathing and heart rate. I also take blood samples and send them to the lab where they are checked for viruses or infection.

Checking the lungs
Every pup admitted to the hospital undergoes an examination for health problems.

Weighing the seal pup
Barney weighs the seal pup. We need to monitor how well the seals are putting on weight before they can be released.

5:15pm I take fish out of the freezer to defrost for tomorrow's feeds, then clean and shut down the hospital. It is important to follow strict procedures in order to keep the hospital sterile and reduce the risk of infection for both seals and humans. By 6 pm it's time to lock up. It's been a long day, but with increasing pressure on the marine environment the rescue, rehabilitation, and release work will help safeguard the future of Britain's marine mammals.

Resident seals
Seals that are unable to survive in the wild are given a permanent home at the center.

Wetland

Swamps and mangrove forests, salt marshes, and mudflats are strange places, halfway between land and sea. Most are muddy, and some stink of rotting vegetation. But they are very, very important. Wetlands protect the coast from waves and tides, and provide sheltered spawning grounds for shellfish and fish. They offer rich feeding areas for birds, especially long-distance migrants, and also offer a safe haven for many rare plants, insects, frogs, and other creatures. They can even filter out some pollutants. But like all habitats, wetlands are fragile and can be damaged.

Trees on stilts

Forests of mangroves, like this one in Indonesia, cover shorelines throughout the tropics. Their tangled, stilt-like roots trap silt, helping to build up the land. In parts of Asia, almost 70 percent of the mangroves have been cut down to make way for fish- and shrimp-farming ponds, leaving the coast vulnerable to storms and tidal waves.

Wetlands take up about **six percent** of the Earth's land **surface**

Saltwater crocodile

The 16 ft (5 m) American crocodile lives in estuaries and mangrove swamps in Florida. Once threatened by hunting, its numbers are now increasing. However, it still suffers from habitat destruction and illegal hunting.

The Sundarbans **wetlands** contain one of India's biggest **tiger reserves**

Watch

Choking invader

The water hyacinth – a native of tropical America – has become a serious problem worldwide. The plant grows very quickly, choking rivers, lakes, and coastal lagoons. The floating vegetation can cover the entire water surface. This robs other plants of the light they need and starves fish of oxygen.

Dense, fibrous roots absorb oxygen and nutrients from the water.

Disaster in Spain

Workers take poisoned fish from a river near the Coto Doñana National Park in Spain in 1998. The disaster occurred when 177 million cubic feet (5 million cubic meters) of mud containing toxic metals spilled from a sludge pond at a mineral mine. The spill affected rare species such as the gecko lizard, otter, and lynx.

Rare species such as this white stork – as well as the imperial eagle – were threatened.

Innocent victim

A manatee or "sea cow" shows the terrible scars caused by powerboat propellers. This large, slow, gentle plant-eater is found in bays, estuaries, and coastal lagoons in Florida and the Caribbean. It is protected by law, but still suffers from boat injuries, poaching, and even sudden temperature changes.

By 1999, **116 countries** had signed an **international** agreement to **protect** the world's wetlands

Staging post

Thousands of knots (small, plump shorebirds) wheel above the mudflats of East Anglia, England. The birds breed in the Arctic tundra but fly south to spend the winter on the coasts of western Europe and even as far south as West Africa. Coastal wetlands like these are vital feeding areas for many types of migrant birds.

66 I live in a remote village on the Norfolk coast in England. The village overlooks salt marshes where the Norfolk Wildlife Trust has a bird reserve. Here people can watch rare birds from hides (small huts with peepholes). Sadly, the birds' homes are under threat from strong tides breaking through the shingle bank and flooding the marshes, the roads, and people's homes. Some people make a living by cutting down reeds that grow in the marsh. These are used to thatch roofs. 99

J. W. G. Groom

OCEANS AT RISK

> 66 The reality is that my country's pollution needs no visa to visit your country – just a favorable current. 99

ROBERT HILL
FEDERAL ENVIRONMENT MINISTER, AUSTRALIA

MORE POLLUTION HAS BEEN DUMPED AT SEA IN THE PAST CENTURY THAN IN THE PREVIOUS 2,000 years. The cocktail of sewage, chemicals, oil, nuclear and solid waste is poisoning our coasts and spreading far out into the oceans. Action is needed now – growing populations are set to make the problems worse.

A huge breaker thunders towards Oahu island in Hawaii (main picture). The water looks crystal clear, but even here in the mid-Pacific, far from the world's industrial centers, the ocean contains traces of industrial chemicals that pollute coastal waters and affect fisheries. The smaller picture shows why.

Chemical Pollution

Acid fumes from factory chimneys, pesticides and fertilizers from farmland, and poisons that seep from waste dumps are all types of chemical pollution. At first they do not seem to have much to do with the oceans, which may be hundreds of miles away. However, the land and the sea are linked together by rivers, and by rainwater seeping through the ground. Whatever we spill, throw away, burn, or bury eventually mingles with the water and begins its journey to the sea. These chemicals affect living things in ways that we do not fully understand. For this reason, some governments are now passing laws to try and prevent the dumping of pollutants into the world's waters.

Chemical sprays

Farmers and foresters often spray chemical pesticides to protect their crops and trees from insect pests. The problem is that some of these chemicals remain in the environment long after they have done their job. They get washed into rivers where they damage plant and animal life.

Agro-chemicals
Pesticides and fertilizers can harm the environment.

Acid rain
Chemicals in factory smoke can dissolve in rainwater to form acid rain which damages trees and soil.

Saltwater
When salt is put onto roads in winter, it can wash into rivers and kill the freshwater fish.

Journey to the sea

Some pollutants break down into harmless substances before they ever reach the sea. Others – such as metals from industrial processes and pesticides – build up in the environment. Also, fertilizers, detergents, and sewage add nutrients to the water that cause rapid growth of algae, relatives of the seaweeds. This uses up all the available oxygen which, in turn, kills the fish.

ACTION!
NEVER POLLUTE

Never throw litter, such as cans or plastic bottles, into rivers or seas.

Recycle whatever you can.

Report any colored or smelly river water to the local government.

Fatal food chain

In the 1950s, people living around Minamata Bay in Japan began to fall ill. Many died, and children were born with serious health problems. The cause was methyl mercury, dumped into the bay by a chemical company. The deadly mercury had been absorbed by fish and shellfish, which had then been caught for food by local people.

People are harmed if they eat the poisoned fish or shellfish.

Oysters

Grey mullet

Mercury is discharged into the sea along with waste water.

By law, many **factories** now have to **recycle** their own **waste water**

Thermal pollution
Hot water discharged by power stations can harm local marine life.

No safe place

Pollution is hard to contain. The pesticide DDT has been found in the bodies of Antarctic penguins. This has happened despite the fact that these penguins live far away from where DDT was used, and that it has been banned for 20 years.

Sewage
Untreated sewage flows into the sea, contaminating mud on the coast.

Dumping of **plastic** waste from ships at sea is **banned** by international treaty

Industrial waste
Material dumped at sea may leak and be hazardous to marine life.

Rusting wrecks
Old ships may steadily release pollutants into the sea from their cargo.

Deadly surge

These dead fish litter the banks of the Seine River on the outskirts of Paris after a chemical spill at a factory upriver. But dead fish are only part of the story. The spilt chemicals seep into the mud of the estuary and are absorbed by worms and shellfish – which are in turn eaten by fish and seabirds.

Whatever goes down a drain ends up in the big sink – the ocean

Tainted *waters*

Erosion scars
Stripped of their protective covering of trees, these hills in Madagascar show how rainwater can quickly wash away the soil.

Sometimes pollution is obvious. Rivers near copper and iron mines may be stained by metals seeping from waste dumps. Rivers and shorelines can become covered by frothy scum that forms when chemicals and farm fertilizers run into the water. Too much mud in a river is also a form of pollution because it can choke delicate coastal habitats. But even more deadly is the pollution we cannot see. When dangerous chemicals are spilled or buried on land, they slowly filter into the water deep below the ground. It may take many years, but they eventually end up in rivers – and the sea. We must endeavor to protect the seas from becoming tainted with pollutants.

River of mud
After a night of heavy rain, this river in Haiti stains the sea brown with soil swept off the deforested slopes inland.

Choking reefs
Once beautiful coral reefs are suffocated under a blanket of mud washed down by the river.

Every year, **erosion** robs the **Earth** of 25 billion **tons** more **topsoil** than it produces

Smothering silt

These pictures show the devastating effects of deforestation. All over the world, forests are being cut down to satisfy the demand for hardwoods such as teak and mahogany. They are also cut down to make way for farms, or simply to provide local people with firewood and animal feed. The result is the same – bare hillsides, rivers of mud, dams and irrigation systems silted up, and coastal habitats choked with mud.

Replanting

In parts of the Himalayas, mountain slopes have been stripped bare by people desperate for firewood and foliage to feed to their yaks. This Nepalese woman is planting pine seedlings as part of an international project to repair the damaged hillsides and stop soil erosion.

Blooming algae

Rivers carry farm fertilizers from the land to the sea. When they reach the sea, these chemicals also fertilize algae in the water, causing them to grow faster than usual. The pounding surf beats the jellylike coatings of the algae into a thick, smelly froth, which washes up on our beaches.

TOXIC RUNOFF

EXPERIMENT

You will need: 2 baking trays, a brick, gloves, soil, a trowel, food coloring, water, pitcher, pieces of sod

1 SET UP THE TRAYS as shown in the picture above. Then fill the sloping tray with an even layer of soil and press it down firmly. Half fill the other tray with water.

2 PLANT SMALL PIECES OF SOD in the soil. Let them grow for a few days to provide vegetation cover.

3 MAKE A HOLE IN THE SOIL at the top of the slope, and put in a few drops of food coloring. This is your "illegal" toxic waste dump. Pour water gently onto the soil.

Coloring is washed through the soil by water

4 SWIRLS OF COLOR in the lower baking tray reveal the arrival of the water you poured onto the soil – stained by its unwelcome cargo of "pollution."

This shows that: water can wash toxic pollutants out of "safe storage" on the land into rivers and seas.

ACTION!
CUT POLLUTION

Only use a small amount of liquid detergent when you wash the dishes.

Remember that what you throw on the land can eventually make its way to the sea.

Toxic dump

Nobody wants toxic waste on their doorstep. However, rich industrial nations sometimes illegally dump their waste on poorer countries. Here, waste from Italy leaks into the soil in Koko, Nigeria, poisoning the soil where the villagers grow their crops.

FOUL SEA

People have been throwing domestic and farm waste into the sea for thousands of years. Long ago, when the world's population was only a few million, this was not a big problem. The amount of garbage was small, and the tides and currents soon washed it away. Things are very different now the world population is 6 billion. The amount of trash we are dumping is enormous, and a lot of it is dangerous – industrial chemicals, raw sewage, even nuclear waste. Although international laws limit many types of dumping at sea, there is still much to be done in the campaign for cleaner seas.

A supply of **clean water** is essential for all **life**

A thing of the past

The sea turns orange as a ship dumps hundreds of tons of jarosite (the waste product of zinc smelting) off the coast of Australia in 1990. The last permit for this kind of dumping ran out in 1997. No new permits have been issued for dumping industrial waste in Australia's waters.

Mineral waste dumped at sea can sink and kill life on the sea floor.

San Francisco Bay contains more than 150 **foreign** species carried there in ships' ballast tanks

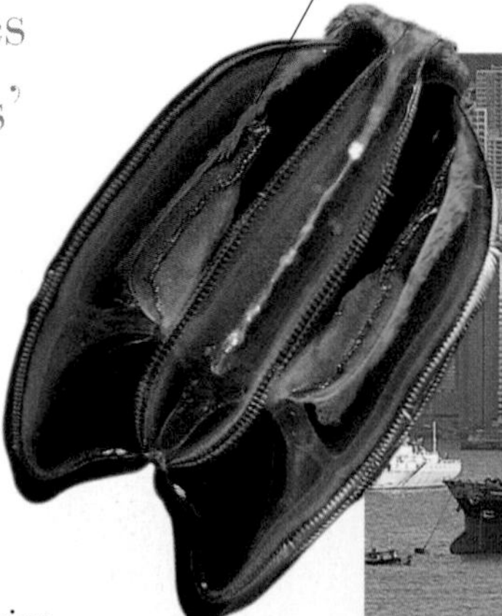

Comb jelly

Alien invaders

When ships unload their cargo, they fill their ballast tanks with seawater to add weight and keep them stable. On arrival at the next port, they pump out the ballast water – teeming with "foreign" marine life. The comb jelly shown here was transported from the North Atlantic to the Black Sea, where it has thrived and upset the local ecosystem.

Drum full of low-level
nuclear waste

Nuclear dumping

This image shows low-level nuclear
waste being dumped in the North Sea.
This type of waste includes clothing
and equipment contaminated with
radioactive chemicals that have been
used in hospitals and research
laboratories. Although dumping
of high-level nuclear waste is
already banned – it still happens.

Piped pollution

All over the world, raw sewage is poured
into the sea. The sewage feeds bacteria
which multiply and deprive other sea
creatures of oxygen. It also contains germs
that can cause diseases. The problem is
worst in developing countries, where there
may be no proper sewage treatment plants.

Bacteria in sewage can
cause **fatal diseases**
such as **cholera**

❝ I live in a village called St. Agnes on the
coast of north Cornwall, England. My life revolves
around surfing and the ocean. I go surfing just
about every day, and it is really important to me
that the sea is kept clean. If it is dirty I am at risk
of getting ill from the pollution and sewage, along with all the
other animals that swim in the water. I try to help by
supporting an environmental group called Surfers
Against Sewage who campaign to clean the seas.
SAS has done a lot for the health of the sea
and for surfers since it was first set up. ❞

Brennan Cascelles

Surfers against sewage

The water off our coasts is sometimes so full of
bacteria from raw sewage that beaches are closed
to the public. Many people campaign to clean up
the seas, but the loudest protests have come
from surfers – the people who suffer most from
illnesses caused by sewage. Their actions have
persuaded many goverments to clean up their acts.

Plastic dumped in the
oceans **kills** an estimated
40,000 **seals** a year

ACTION!
MAKE WAVES

Join an organization that is
campaigning for cleaner seas.

Always find out if water
is clean before
you go swimming in it.

Disaster!

The supertanker *Exxon Valdez* struck a reef in Prince William Sound, Alaska, on March 24, 1989. Eleven million gallons (42 million liters) of crude oil poured into the sea, covering 1,200 miles (2,000 km) of shoreline in a thick, poisonous sludge. People feared that the delicate sea and shoreline habitats would never recover. More than ten years later, the herring schools and harbor seals have not returned, but the salmon are back, and so are the bald eagles, murres, and other seabirds. Slowly, Prince William Sound is beginning to heal.

There have been about **50 oil spills** as big as the *Exxon Valdez* since 1970

Boom time

When the tanker *Sea Empress* ran aground in Milford Haven, Wales, in 1996, about 72,000 tons of oil were spilled. Floating booms like this were used to scoop up about 2,000 tons of the oil before it could drift onto the shore. About 36,000 tons of oil were dispersed at sea using chemicals sprayed from aircraft.

It takes **years** for coastal **fisheries** to recover from a **major oil spill**

Lightening the load

With the *Exxon Valdez* stuck on Bligh Reef, the disaster team rushed smaller tankers to the scene to pump out 42 million gallons (160 million liters) of oil still in the tanks. This reduced the threat of further spills. It also lightened the tanker so that it could be towed off the reef.

The big cleanup

After the disaster, it took a massive effort to clean up. An army of 11,000 people, many volunteers, toiled for weeks with high-pressure water jets, rakes, shovels, even paper towels, to mop up oil from the rocks. But nature is the best cleaner. Most of the oil was broken up and washed away by the waves, tides, and currents.

Escort ships now **watch** over **every tanker** as it passes through **Prince William Sound**

Natural protection

A bird feather consists of hundreds of fine strands held together by hooks, or barbules. When a seabird is coated in oil, the hooks are "undone." This ruins the feather's waterproofing and the bird may die. It can take two hours to clean the oil off a single bird.

Counting the cost

Scientists can only guess how many birds and mammals died in the *Exxon Valdez* spill. It is always difficult to separate the direct effects of an oil spill from natural fluctuations caused by diseases and other factors.

Killer whales
About 20 died, probably from eating fish contaminated with oil.

Sea otters
Up to 5,000 died. Many also left because of local food shortages.

Harbor seals
Up to 300 died. The figures could be higher as seals sink when dead.

Seabirds
Up to half a million died. Some species are still not recovering.

OIL AND FEATHERS

You will need: rubber gloves, a plate, water, 2 bunches of bird feathers, cooking oil, cotton balls, liquid detergent.

1 POUR A LITTLE water onto a plate. Pour some oil onto the surface. Dip both bunches of feathers into the oily water to imitate what happens when a seabird lands on an oil slick in the sea.

Wear gloves when handling feathers.

2 CLEAN ONE BUNCH of feathers using just water and cotton balls. Clean the other bunch using water mixed with liquid detergent.

Feathers cleaned with water

Feathers cleaned with liquid detergent

3 EXAMINE THE FEATHERS. Those cleaned with water alone are still matted and heavy. The others are cleaner and lighter.

This shows that: washing an oiled bird with water and dish detergent gives it the best chance. Even so, cleaned birds can still die of cold.

MARINE IMPACT SPECIALIST
DR. JULIAN GALLOWAY

JULIAN GALLOWAY TRAVELS ALL OVER THE WORLD FOR HIS JOB. HIS WORK INVOLVES LOOKING AT HOW DEVELOPMENTS, SUCH AS PORTS AND HARBORS, or structures including oil and gas platforms, will affect the local environment. His years of training as an oceanographer help him to carry out these studies.

Oil tanker
A tanker unloads its cargo of oil at a jetty. Any oil spill can harm sea life.

A day in the life of a
MARINE IMPACT SPECIALIST

As the coasts come under increasing pressure from developers, it is often scientists who can help to limit any damage to the environment.

Julian has just flown from the UK, arriving in Bangkok early in the morning. He has come to study the effect on the local environment of a new port that might be built in the Gulf of Thailand.

Koh Samet beach
Tropical beaches attract tourists and valuable income to Thailand so they need to be protected.

5:30am First thing I do on arrival is to collect several pieces of marine survey equipment at the airport. Then I drive to Rayong on the Gulf of Thailand to meet up with colleagues. We load the current meter, water quality-testing instruments, and seabed scanners onto a local boat. Because it is quite a drop down from the jetty to the boat, we tie ropes around the boxes and two of us lower the equipment.

7:30am Before leaving, we test the equipment on the boat. We then sail about 2.5 miles (4 km) down the coast to a jetty where ships unload cargoes of oil and fish. This is where two more jetties and a breakwater – to create a new port – might be built.

9:00am We begin collecting water samples from the sea surface using special bottles. These will be sent back to the laboratory in the UK. Scientists will measure

Map of Thailand
Rayong is an important area for tourism as well as nature conservation.

the amount of oil, toxic metals, and other chemicals that indicate pollution levels. I use a special piece of equipment (called a multi-parameter probe) to measure the temperature and saltiness of the sea. It also measures levels of oxygen and sediment (loose material). The information will help me understand the health of local coral reefs and fish. To take these readings, I attach a probe to a

Current meter
This measures the speed and direction of water movement.

> **"My work draws together many different skills – biology, geology, engineering, and oceanography."**

small computer using a waterproof cable. Then I tie a weight to the probe, and use a rope to lower it into the water. I take measurements at the sea surface, and at every 3.3 ft (1 meter) of depth. Meanwhile, my colleagues check water movement with a current meter.

10:30am Next we measure the shape of the seabed with an echo sounder and side-scan sonar. This will help us study how sediments move near the coral reef. The echo sounder looks straight down to the seabed, but the side-scan sonar looks out at an angle. The sonar is called a "fish" because it has fins to help it travel smoothly through the water. Because the "fish" is very heavy, we lower it into the water with a winch and cable.

11:30am We move on to a well-known coral reef called Koh Samet. Tourists go there to watch the reef fish and admire the shapes and

Dredger at work
Dredging the water stirs up sediment in the water, which can kill coral and force fish to move elsewhere.

colors of the corals. Once there, we use an underwater video camera to film the fish and corals. Later we will use the video tape to make a list of all the fish and corals we have seen. This helps us understand the range of marine life in the area.

1:00pm We stop work for lunch on the boat. I study the information on water quality, seabed shape, fish, and coral reef. This will help me plan the new port with least impact on the marine ecosystem. For example, we may need to take into account seasonal currents when dredging. I'm worried that dredgers could disturb sand on the seabed. The reef could be killed, with important fish moving away from the area. I decide to travel to a nearby port to study how that was built.

4:00pm Map Ta Phut Port is down the coast from Rayong. The planned new port will be similar to this one. After studying the port area, I meet the people in charge and talk about how they intend to build the new one. I tell them I am worried about the coral reef, and that the local environment protection department should be

Desolate beach
Construction work scars a beach, but with good planning it can be restored.

told. The managers explain that the new port is important as it will provide vital jobs for local people. They also tell me that the fish industry is a big employer because nam pla – a fish paste used in Thai cooking – is made in Rayong.

5:00pm We travel back to our hotel very tired. I use my computer to predict what the sediment disturbance might be on the reef and fish. I was right to be worried – a lot of sand could fall on the reef and damage the coral. This is because sand stops light, which coral needs to survive, from getting through. I test a new way of building the port. This time my computer shows the sediment moving harmlessly away from the reef. With care, and new building methods, the port could be built with no damage to the reef and fish. Pleased that the local people may have new jobs at a new port, make fish paste, and enjoy the coral reef, I sit down to write up my report.

Underwater camera
Counting fish and coral species is easier when they are recorded on video.

Life in the coral
The reefs in the shallow waters off Thailand are among the richest in the world.

Side-scan sonar
This instrument uses sound waves to map the shape of the seabed.

A major sea level rise could affect 72 million people in China alone

RISING SEA LEVELS

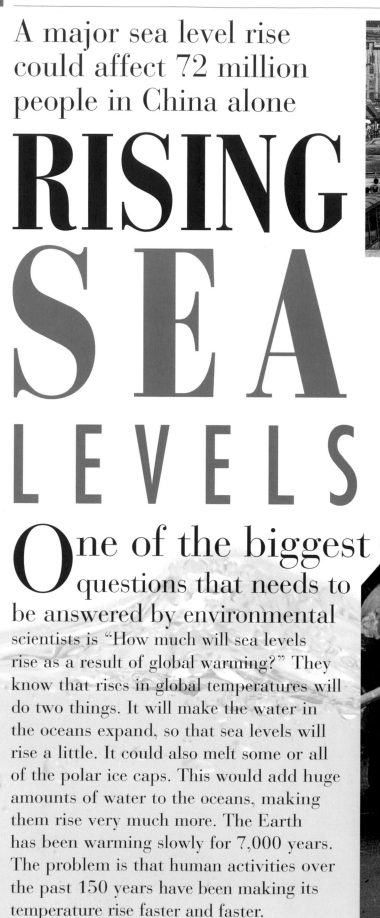

Global warming

Carbon dioxide, water vapor, and methane are the main "greenhouse" gases. Like the panes of a greenhouse, they let the Sun's energy (and heat) in, and then trap some of it. Without them, we would freeze. But vehicle exhausts, factory emissions, and forest burning have added too much extra. The greenhouse is now too efficient, and the Earth is overheating.

One of the biggest questions that needs to be answered by environmental scientists is "How much will sea levels rise as a result of global warming?" They know that rises in global temperatures will do two things. It will make the water in the oceans expand, so that sea levels will rise a little. It could also melt some or all of the polar ice caps. This would add huge amounts of water to the oceans, making them rise very much more. The Earth has been warming slowly for 7,000 years. The problem is that human activities over the past 150 years have been making its temperature rise faster and faster.

Cracks in the ice

Over the past few years, huge chunks have broken away from the floating ice shelves around Antarctica. The cause is a rise in sea temperature – and it is a serious warning to us all. When floating ice melts, sea levels do not change. But if the ice caps that cover land start to melt, the world is in trouble because sea levels will rise.

MELTING ICE CAPS

EXPERIMENT

You will need: 2 identical glass bowls, tray, 2 unopened food cans, pitcher, water, ice cubes, marker tape.

1 PLACE THE BOWLS on a tray with a can inside each one. Part fill the first bowl with water, add plenty of ice, and mark the water level with tape. Mark the same level on the second bowl and fill up to the mark with water.

2 PILE ICE CUBES on top of the can in the second bowl, but do not put any ice in the water. You have created one "island" surrounded by "sea ice" and one covered by an "ice cap."

3 LEAVE THE ICE to melt. Notice that the water level in the first bowl is the same, but the "sea level" in the second bowl has risen.

This shows that: when sea ice melts, the water does not take up any extra volume. But when land ice melts, water levels rise.

Parts of **London**, England, could **flood** if sea levels **rise** 10 ft (3 m)

Florida's rising sea levels

Low-lying coastal areas around the world are at risk from sea level rise. In Florida (left) a rise of 25 ft (7.5 m) would swamp vast areas of the state, including Miami and West Palm Beach. Elsewhere in the world, cities such as Amsterdam, Bombay, and Sydney would vanish beneath the water.

The flood threat

Millions of Bangladeshis in the lowlands of the Ganges delta suffer from flooding caused by monsoon rains and hurricanes. If sea levels rise, millions of acres of their low-lying coastal farmland could disappear forever under a shallow, salty sea.

GEORGIA
ATLANTIC OCEAN
FLORIDA
Cape Canaveral
GULF OF MEXICO
The Everglades
West Palm Beach
Miami

☐ Florida coastline
☐ Florida after flooding
Florida Keys

Half the **world's population** lives in **low-lying coastal** areas

Sea defenses

Low-lying, developed countries, such as the Netherlands, already spend huge amounts of money building sea defenses. These walls prevent seawater from spilling onto the land. If sea levels rise they will need to be far higher and cover longer stretches of coast.

Seawall under construction

Action Plan

IF YOU CARE ABOUT THE OCEANS and want to help save their natural environment, there are many organizations that will help to get you involved. This list includes those you can contact in the US, as well as international organizations you can visit on the internet.

American Bird Conservancy
Dedicated to the conservation of wild birds and their habitats. This website has information and campaigns about current issues such as the effect of climate change on birds.

www.abcbirds.org

PO Box 249
The Plains
VA 20198

American Society for the Prevention of Cruelty to Animals (ASPCA)
National charity involved in all aspects of animal welfare. The site has a kids section with information and ideas for school projects.

www.aspca.org

424 East 92nd Street
New York, New York 10128

BBC Nature
A website with news, tv program follow-ups, competitions, events, and factfiles all relating to the natural world.

www.bbc.co.uk/nature

BBC Science
Information about the oceans and marine science, from climate-change threats and coral reefs to pollution.

www.bbc.co.uk/science

British Antarctic Survey
An organization responsible for the UK's scientific research in Antarctica and the Antarctic Ocean. The website gives full details of current research programs.

www.antarctica.ac.uk

High Cross
Madingley Road
Cambridge CB3 0ET
UK

California Coastal Conservancy
An organization that helps preserve, protect, and restore the resources of the California Coast.

www.coastalconservancy.ca.gov

1330 Broadway
11th Floor
Oakland
CA 94612

Center for Marine Conservation
Runs programs and campaigns ranging from shark conservation to protection of coral reefs. The website contains links to many organizations involved in marine conservation.

www.cmc-ocean.org

The Coral Reef Alliance
Promotes coral reef conservation around the world by supporting protection efforts and raising public awareness.

www.coral.org

2014 Shattuck Avenue
Berkeley
CA 94704

The Cousteau Society
Jacques Cousteau and his team have led the way for underwater exploration and discovery. The Society promotes protection and improvement of sea life for future generations.

www.cousteausociety.org

870 Greenbrier Circle, Suite 402
Chesapeake, VA 23320

Environmental Investigation Agency
An international organization committed to investigating environmental crime and changing the laws that protect endangered species and habitats.

www.eia-international.org

69 Old Street
London EC1V 9HX
UK

Friends of the Earth
International network of environmental groups that commissions research and campaigns for changes in the law.

www.foei.org

1025 Vermont Ave, NW
3rd floor
Washington, DC 20005-6303

Great American Fish Count
A US-based program that makes use of volunteer divers to study fish populations and marine habitats and makes this information available to the public and researchers alike.

www.fishcount.org/information/information.html

Greenpeace
One of the world's major environmental organizations, involved in direct action to safeguard the planet's future.

www.greenpeace.org

International Tsunami Information Center
Special division of the US National Weather Service, providing information about tsunamis.

www.shoa.cl/oceano/itic/frontpage.html

International Union for the Conservation of Nature and Natural Resources (IUCN)
The world's largest conservation-related organization that brings together 76 states and many other groups in a unique worldwide partnership.

www.iucn.org

National Audubon Society
Concerned with conserving and restoring natural ecosystems for birds and other wildlife, for the benefit of the Earth and people.

www.audubon.org

PO Box 52529
Boulder, CO 80322-2529

Project Seahorse
Program of seahorse management, involving community action, practical conservation, and scientific study of seahorses and their habitats.

www.projectseahorse.org

Seaweb
Web-based project where you can find all the latest news stories about the ocean environment.

www.seaweb.org

Surfers Against Sewage
Active grassroots campaign to stop marine sewage and toxic waste discharge into waters around Britain.

www.sas.org.uk

2 Rural Workshops
Wheal Kitty
St Agnes
Cornwall TR5 0RD
UK

Tourism Concern
Promotes awareness of tourism's impact on people and their environments, and campaigns for a fair distribution of the benefits from tourism.

www.tourismconcern.org.uk

Stapleton House
277-281 Holloway Road
London N7 8HN
UK

United Nations Environment Programme (UNEP)
The UN agency founded in 1972 to safeguard and enhance the environment for the benefit of present and future generations.

www.unep.org

United Nations Avenue, Gigiri
PO Box 30552,
Nairobi, Kenya

United States Environmental Protection Agency
US government agency which aims to protect human health and to safeguard the natural environment – air, water, and land – upon which life depends.

www.epa.gov

United States Fish and Wildlife Service
Helps protect a healthy environment for fish, wildlife, and people. Main interests are migratory birds, endangered species, marine mammals, freshwater and migratory fish.

www.fws.gov

Department of the Interior
1849 C Street NW
Washington, DC 20240

World Conservation Monitoring Centre
Collects and publishes information about the world's endangered species, as well as environmental issues such as climate change, coral bleaching, and sea level change. Try the searchable database at the WCMC website.

www.wcmc.org.uk

219 Huntingdon Road
Cambridge CB3 0DL
UK

Worldwide Fund for Nature (WWF)
The world's largest international conservation organization. Visit the website to find out about what the WWF does and to check out the Living Plant Report.

www.panda.org

1250 24th St NW
PO Box 97180
Washington, DC 20037-1175

Index

Credits

Dorling Kindersley would like to thank:
Sheila Hanly for locating many of the Day in the Life experts; Amanda Carroll, Sheila Collins, Sharon Grant, Claire Legemah, Keith Newell, Peter Radcliffe, and Laura Roberts for design help; Lynn Bresler, index.

Andy Crawford for photography of the experiments, and models Harriet Couchman and Dejaune Davis.

Special thanks to Day in the Life experts and their organizations who provided many free photographs – Carl Meyer (Marine Biologist); Keith Saunders (Fisheries Protection Officer); Amanda Vincent (Seahorse Specialist); Keiran Copeland (Marine Mammal Medic); Julian Galloway (Marine Impact Specialist). Thanks to the AOC, REEF, and US NOAA Marine Sanctuary Program.

Additional photography: Geoff Brightling, Jane Burton, Steve Gorton, Frank Greenaway, Dave King, Ray Moller, Andreas von Einsiedel, Alex Wilson. Models: Martin Camm, Peter Griffiths, Peter Minister.

Picture Credits

The publishers would like to thank the following for their kind permission to reproduce the photographs:
a = above; c = center; b = bottom; l = left; r = right; t = top; f = far; n = near.

Heather Angel: 15bc. **Ardea London Ltd:** 43c; Chris Knights 43bl; Hans D. Dossenbach 37bl; John Mason 21br; K.W. Fink 53bl. **Tomas Bertelsen:** 34tl. **Bruce Coleman Ltd:** 12, 32b; Derek Croucher 36b; Fred Bruemmer 32br; Gerald S. Cubitt 42l; John Cancalosi 33c, 33br, 37cb; Mark N. Boulton 36–37t; Neil McAllister 31cl; Nicholas Devore 46tr; Thomas Buchholz 54bl. **Colorific!:** Philippe Hays 57br. **© Crown Copyright: Historic Royal Palaces 1999:** 15t. **DK Picture Library:** Apple Macintosh 18cr. Brad Doane: 22b. **Edgetech:** 55br. **Environmental Images:** 49bl; Alex Olah 49tl; Chris Martin 26tr; Daniel Beltra 43tl; David Hoffman 47cbl; Herbert Girardet 56cr; Peter Rowlands 23br; Pierre Gleizes 51tr; Richard Smith 38tl; Roger Grace 31tr; Steve Morgan 20cl, 20bc, 57tl. **Greenpeace Inc:** Hewetson 50-51; Matoff 11bl. **Robert Harding Picture Library:** 33tr; Guy Thouvenin 33bl. **Hutchison Library:** 47tc. **Hyder Consulting:** 54tl, 54br, 54-55, 55tl, 55cl. **Image Bank:** Paul McCormick 37br. **Institute of Marine Biology, Hawaii:** 18tl, 18-19, 19tr, 19cl. **Japanese Meteorological Agency/Meteorological Office:** 14tr, 14tcl, 14tcr. **Kos Pictures Source:** Gilles Martin-Raget 38-39b. **FLPA - Images of Nature:** D. P. Wilson 47cl; Ron Austing 14cr. **Jessica Meeuwig, Research Scientist, Project Seahorse:** 34bl. **Don Merton:** 33cl. **Natural History Museum, London:** 7br. **N.H.P.A.:** John Shaw 42cbr; Norbert Wu 16clb, 22-23; Roger Tidman 40-41. **Oxford Scientific Films:** Doug Allan 48tl; John Brown 13tl; Laurence Gould 8t; Mark Webster 30-31; Michael Pitts 50br. **Panos Pictures:** R.Berriedale-Johnson 38bl. **Planet Earth Pictures:** 12-13; C. Maddock 27cr; Chris Prior 32-33tl; Darroch Donald 53cb; Doug Perrine 43cr; Gary Bell 2-3;

Ivor Edmonds 16cr; Jeannie Mackinnon 48bl; Kurt Amsler 28-29; Norbert Wu 50cb; Patrick de Wilde 13br; Richard Chesher 15cr; Warren Williams 51tl. **Rex Features:** 23tr. **Michael Ricketts:** 34br. **Keith Saunders, Fisheries Western Australia:** 24tl, 24cl, 24bl, 24-25, 25tr, 25cr. **Science Photo Library:** Astrid & Hanns-Frieder Michler 16tl; Douglas Faulkner 6-7, 28-29; Gene Feldman 16tr; Martin Bond 13cr; Vanessa Vick 53cl. **SOS Seal Rescue Hospital, Hunstanton:** 40tl, 40cb, 40br, 41tr, 41cla, 41crb, 41bl. **Still Pictures:** Al Grillo 53tl; Dylan Garcia 45bl; Fred Dott 26-27; Hanson Carroll 17cl; Hartmut Schwarzbach 56cr; Jean-Luc Zeigler 47bl; Kelvin Aitken 39c; Marilyn Kazmers 31cr; Mark Edwards 48cl; Nigel Dickinson 15cr; Norbert Wu 53bc, 53bc; Ray Pfortner 37cl; Roland Seitre 39tr; Ron Giling 22l; Somboon-Unep 27cr; Thomas Raupach 49cl; Yves Lefevre 19b. **Tony Stone Images:** Art Wolfe 21cl; Bob Torrez 51cr; David Woodfall 52l; Norbert Wu 6tl, 10-11; Warren Bolster 7tr, 44-45. **Amanda Vincent, Project Seahorse:** 34crb, 34-35, 35cl, 35cr. **Chris Woods:** National Institute of Water and Atmosphere Research, Wellington, New Zealand 35b.

Jacket Credits

Environmental Images: Richard Smith front bl; Roger Grace front bc. **Robert Harding Picture Library:** Back bc. **N.H.P.A.:** A.N.T front c. **Oxford Scientific Films:** John Brown back clb. **Science Photo Library:** Douglas Faulkner inside back; Gene Feldman/NASA GSFC back cla. **Still Pictures:** Dylan Garcia back cra; Marilyn Kazmers back bl. **Tony Stone Images:** Art Wolfe inside front; Steve Barnett front br.